HAL•LEONARD

INSTRUMENTAL
PLAY-ALONG

AUDIO
ACCESS
INCLUDED

FLUTE

# QUEEN

## UPDATED EDITION

T0081885

**PLAYBACK+**

Speed • Pitch • Balance • Loop

To access audio visit:
**www.halleonard.com/mylibrary**

Enter Code
**3514-3458-4754-3638**

© Jorgen Angel/CTSIMAGES

Audio arrangements by Peter Deneff

ISBN 978-1-5400-3838-8

Contact Us:
**Hal Leonard**
7777 West Bluemound Road
Milwaukee, WI 53213
Email: info@halleonard.com

In Europe contact:
**Hal Leonard Europe Limited**
42 Wigmore Street
Marylebone, London, W1U 2RN
Email: info@halleonardeurope.com

In Australia contact:
**Hal Leonard Australia Pty. Ltd.**
4 Lentara Court
Cheltenham, Victoria, 3192 Australia
Email: info@halleonard.com.au

# ANOTHER ONE BITES THE DUST

FLUTE

Words and Music by
JOHN DEACON

# CRAZY LITTLE THING CALLED LOVE

**Flute**

Words and Music by
FREDDIE MERCURY

# BICYCLE RACE

FLUTE

Words and Music by
FREDDIE MERCURY

D.S. al Coda

CODA

rit.  ff

# BOHEMIAN RHAPSODY

**FLUTE**

Words and Music by
FREDDIE MERCURY

**Hard Rock Shuffle** (♩♩ = ♩♪)

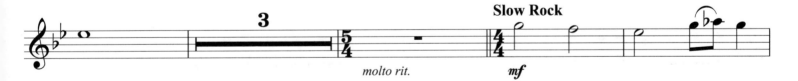

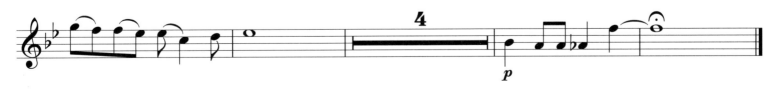

# FAT BOTTOMED GIRLS

**FLUTE**

Words and Music by
BRIAN MAY

# I WANT IT ALL

FLUTE

Words and Music by FREDDIE MERCURY,
BRIAN MAY, ROGER TAYLOR
and JOHN DEACON

# DON'T STOP ME NOW

**FLUTE**

Words and Music by
FREDDIE MERCURY

**D.S. al Coda**

**CODA**

# I WANT TO BREAK FREE

FLUTE

Words and Music by
JOHN DEACON

# PLAY THE GAME

FLUTE

Words and Music by
FREDDIE MERCURY

# KILLER QUEEN

FLUTE

Words and Music by
FREDDIE MERCURY

15

# RADIO GA GA

FLUTE

Words and Music by
ROGER TAYLOR

# SAVE ME

FLUTE

Words and Music by
BRIAN MAY

# SOMEBODY TO LOVE

FLUTE

Words and Music by
FREDDIE MERCURY

# UNDER PRESSURE

Flute

Words and Music by FREDDIE MERCURY,
JOHN DEACON, BRIAN MAY,
ROGER TAYLOR and DAVID BOWIE

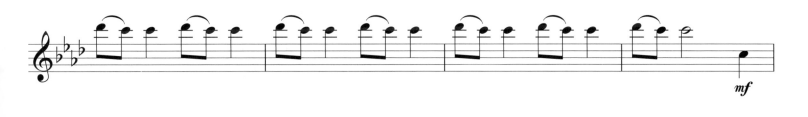

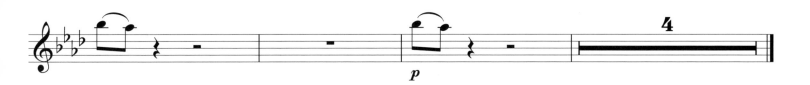

# WE ARE THE CHAMPIONS

Words and Music by
FREDDIE MERCURY

Flute

# WE WILL ROCK YOU

Flute

Words and Music by
BRIAN MAY

# YOU'RE MY BEST FRIEND

FLUTE

Words and Music by
JOHN DEACON